This book belongs to :

..............................

..............................

..............................

This book is dedicated to our little arrows:
Ethan, Allyson, Elijah,
Vanessa and Tiffany

Copyright © 2023 by Joy Sukadi and Lilyana Margaretha
All rights reserved. No part of this publication may be reproduced, stored in retrieval system, or transmitted in any form or by any means, electronic, mechanical, photocopying, recording, or otherwise, without written permission of the publisher.

*Sulley the Seal Learns to Surf* / by Joy Sukadi and Lilyana Margaretha
ISBN: 978-1-7376802-5-3

Published by:
Sharpening Little Arrows, LLC
www.SharpeningLittleArrows.com

*Kids' beginner guide to safe internet surfing*

# Sulley the Seal
## Learns to Surf

Written by: Joy Sukadi
and Lilyana Margaretha

Once upon a wave in the heart of Hawaii, there lived a happy young seal named Sulley. Along with his parents, Sulley's water adventures unfolded in the colorful and charming little surf town of North Shore, Oahu.

Growing up, he spent a lot of time on the beach—building sand castles, collecting crabs, and helping tiny turtles cross safely into the big blue. He would play the whole day from sunrise till sunset.

***Musubi** is a popular snack and lunch food in Hawaii. It is made with a base of packed rice with meat or fish on top and wrapped with a piece of seaweed.*

Mama Sandy would watch Sulley from the kitchen while making musubi* for lunch. After a long day of work, Papa Stan would rush to the beach to join Sulley. Sulley, with a heart full of happiness, would often whisper to himself, "My life is INCREDIBLE! It could not get any better than this!"

Even though Sulley's island life was totally awesome, there was just one thing he couldn't stop thinking about: **SURFING**!

"Not yet, Sulley. Just wait until you're a bit older," Mama Sandy and Papa Stan always reminded him.

Everyone in the North Shore LOVED surfing! They rode waves all day, did amazing tricks, and had super cool boards. They could never get enough of it. Sulley could not wait to grow up and learn some tricks of his own.

"When can I get my own surfboard, Dad?" Sulley asked one day.

Almost choking on his coffee, Papa Stan put down his mug. "When you grow older, kiddo. This ocean is a beautiful place full of wonderful things to discover. But if we are not careful, we can be…"

"I know, I know," Sulley replied.

"SHARK FOOD!" Both of them exclaimed at the same time.

"You got it, bud!" Papa Stan nudged Sulley's side, almost knocking his glasses off him.

Sulley grew up with the same activities that all normal seals did: school, homework, beach, musubi, *repeat*.

However, one afternoon, just before his 13th birthday, he came home from school looking a little sad. "What's wrong, buddy?" Mama Sandy asked while taking a steaming-hot baked salmon out of the oven.

"Mom, ALL of my friends have their own surfboards," Sulley could barely hide his frustration. "They ride the waves for hours after school. I'm the only one in class WITHOUT a surfboard. It makes me feel really left out!"

"Oh, honey, I know how it feels to be the odd one out. It's tough. But surfing in the open ocean is NOT SAFE! Do you know that the ocean is full of dangerous and hungry predators that are targeting you? You could be their next meal!" Mama Sandy explained.

Papa Stan walked into the kitchen after overhearing the conversation. "Son, I know you've waited for this moment your whole life, but please give us time to think. We just want to make sure that you're safe."

"Dad, I'll be safe, I promise! You can teach me everything about surfing, and I'll follow your lead. Just tell me how!"

Papa Stan cleared his throat and spoke sternly, "It's not that we don't trust you, kiddo. It's the predators out there we're worried about. But I'll talk to your mom about it tonight, okay?"

Later that night…

"This is it, hon." Mama Sandy sighed heavily. "The day we've been worried about is finally here. Our little one wants his own surfboard!" She closed her eyes. A vivid image of seals' fins being chomped off by sharks flashed through her mind. "He's defenseless," she shuddered.

"Honey, this might sound a bit crazy. I know we've promised to wait until he's older for a surfboard, but hear me out." Papa Stan cleared his throat. "We have two choices: One, we get him a surfboard now, and I'll teach him EVERYTHING about ocean safety. I'll coach him myself."

Papa Stan paused for a moment. "Option two is to NOT let him surf at all to keep him safe. But think again. Sooner or later, he will have to learn how to surf on his own. Besides, how can we be sure he won't surf behind our backs with his friends' boards?"

"You made a good point," Mama Sandy said, looking at her husband's concerned face. "Let's be reasonable now. One day, he's going to surf all day, all week. He even wants to be a surfboard maker when he grows up!"

After a deep breath, she finally made up her mind. "I can't believe I'm saying this, but I prefer the first option. We'll surf and navigate together as a family, teaching him all he needs to know about ocean safety…"

"…we *do* have a few years to coach and train him to be a safe and responsible surfer," Mama Sandy said, as if trying to convince herself.

"So, can we **seal** the deal?" Papa Stan gave her a playful, teasing look.

Mama Sandy laughed aloud. "Oh, don't be **seal-ly**! What would I do without you?"

On the morning of his 13th birthday, Sulley could smell the baked musubi cake his mom always made on his special day.
"**MUSUBI!**" Sulley exclaimed as he dashed into the kitchen.

There, leaning against the wall, was a huge present, even taller than Papa Stan! Sulley's eyes lit up.
"Mom, Dad, is it what I think it is?"

"Open it up, kiddo," Mama Sandy smiled while holding onto her husband's fin a little too tightly.

"Relax, honey. We've got this," Papa Stan reassured her, gently patting her fin.

Sulley rushed to open his birthday present, revealing the famous pineapple surfboard he'd always dreamed of! "Whoa! Thanks, Mom and Dad! You're the absolute best!" Sulley exclaimed, rushing over to give his parents a tight, seal-sized hug.

The next day, Mama Sandy and Papa Stan took Sulley to the beach for his first-ever surfing lesson. He was bursting with excitement! After all, his parents had been riding waves for 20 years. They must know a thing or two about the ocean!

"Son, **Rule #1: Always surf with a buddy *inside* the reef boundaries. Never go alone beyond these limits.**"

"Some families might allow their kids to do this, but not us. This is crucial for your safety. The open ocean can be dangerous when you surf on your own. No one can save you if something bad happens.
So, stay within the safe boundaries."

"**Rule #2: Do not surf at night when it's dark.** Even if it seems fun and your friends are out there after 9 PM, it's not safe. It's hard to see where you're going, and there might be predators hunting for food."

"A lot of things can go wrong when you ignore these two rules. Kids surfing alone, in the dark, are easy prey for predators. We trust you, but we don't trust them," Papa Stan emphasized. Sulley nodded, listening closely.

Mama Sandy chimed in, "So, can you sneak out to surf when Mom and Dad are asleep?"

"No, ma'am!" Sulley replied quickly. "We surf together in broad daylight. Got it!"

So far, so good. Papa Stan continued, "**Rule #3: There is no privacy when it comes to surfing.** I know you're a big kid and want independence, but safety comes first. We'll keep a close eye on you, tracking your every move in the ocean. This is *not* an invasion of privacy. It is a **safety measure**."

"Young seals can be in danger when they surf without adult supervision," Mama Sandy explained. "That's why we're going to use a tracking device on you. It'll help us know where you're surfing and if you're ever in danger, especially when we're not around."

Papa Stan got their surfboards ready. "Once you understand these rules and promise to follow them, we can have some fun out there! Are you ready?"

"Yes, sir!" Sulley exclaimed eagerly.

"Now, before we hit the water, let's practice popping up on the board," Papa Stan began his instructions.

**SURFING 101**
1. Wait and watch for a wave
2. Face the shore
3. Lie down on your stomach on the board
4. Paddle, paddle, paddle
5. Pop up & balance!

Sulley and his parents spent the rest of the day enjoying their surfing time together, riding off into the sunset.

Kids, remember these **RULES** for internet and phone safety:

### 1. Always surf with a buddy within your family's boundaries.

Use your phone, tablet, or computer where others can see your screen. Pick a family spot where you can "surf" together as a family, such as the dining table, kitchen counter, or study area. Talk with your family about which apps are okay and which ones are off-limits.

### 2. Do not surf in the dark.

Do not bring your devices into your bedroom at night. Before bedtime, turn them off and charge them in a common area (or in your parents' bedroom). This will keep you away from nighttime predators.

### 3. When it comes to online safety, there's no such thing as privacy.

Expect your parents to read your texts, track your online activity, know your apps, and be aware of your whereabouts. It's not an invasion of privacy; it's about keeping you safe.

## TIPS FOR PARENTS

Before letting your kids "surf" on their own, here are a few tips to follow, just like in the real surfing experience:

**1. Equip your beginner with the right tools.**

Consider getting them a "dumb phone" designed solely for texting and calling parents. These phones have essential features and are ideal for beginners.

## 2. Establish a safe "surfing" territory.

Clearly define what's allowed and what's off-limits for your beginner surfer. For example, limit them to calling/texting parents and taking pictures. Most social media and video-sharing platforms aren't safe for young children.

## 3. Do plenty of land simulations and drills together.

Sit down with your kids and teach them how to use certain apps safely. To maintain accountability, sync your kids' phones with yours. This way, you can monitor their device usage, track which apps they install or remove, and ensure their safety online.

**HAPPY SURFING!**

Made in the USA
Middletown, DE
24 November 2023